DISCARDED

JS77.44

WILD AMERICA
HABITATS

PRAIRIES

By Melissa Cole

BLACKBIRCH®
PRESS

THOMSON

GALE

San Diego • Detroit • New York • San Francisco • Cleveland • New Haven, Conn. • Waterville, Maine • London • Munich

© 2003 by Blackbirch Press™. Blackbirch Press™ is an imprint of The Gale Group, Inc., a division of Thomson Learning, Inc.

Blackbirch Press™ and Thomson Learning™ are trademarks used herein under license.

For more information, contact
The Gale Group, Inc.
27500 Drake Rd.
Farmington Hills, MI 48331-3535
Or you can visit our Internet site at http://www.gale.com

ALL RIGHTS RESERVED
No part of this work covered by the copyright hereon may be reproduced or used in any form or by any means—graphic, electronic, or mechanical, including photocopying, recording, taping, Web distribution, or information storage retrieval systems—without the written permission of the publisher.

Every effort has been made to trace the owners of copyrighted material.

Photo Credits: Cover, all photos © Tom and Pat Leeson Wildlife Photography; pages 20, 23 illustrations by Chris Jouan Illustration

LIBRARY OF CONGRESS CATALOGING-IN-PUBLICATION DATA

Cole, Melissa S.
  Prairies / by Melissa S. Cole.
    p. cm. — (Wild America habitats series)
Summary: Discusses the grasses, plants, animals, climate, food, water, humans, and ecology of the prairie.
Includes bibliographical references and index.
  ISBN 1-56711-807-0 (hardback : alk. paper)
  1. Prairie ecology—Juvenile literature. [1. Grasslands. 2. Prairies. 3. Prairie ecology. 4. Ecology.] I. Title. II. Series.

QH541.5.P7C56 2003
577.4'4—dc21   2002010368

Printed in China
10 9 8 7 6 5 4 3 2 1

Contents

Introduction 4
Where Are Prairies Found Today? 7
What Makes Prairies Unique? 8
Prairie Plants 10
Prairie Animals 14
Food Chain 20
Humans and Prairies 21
A Prairie's Food Web 23

Introduction

Prairies are one of the many habitats found in North America. A habitat is an area where certain plants and animals live together. Prairies are large, open fields with many kinds of grasses and wildflowers, but few trees. Prairies usually grow between mountains and forests.

So much rain falls on tall-grass prairies that some grasses grow up to 10 feet high.

Where Are Prairies Found Today?

Prairies are found in three major regions. The short-grass prairie begins at the foot of the Colorado Rocky Mountains. It stretches eastward to the western edge of Kansas. This area receives very little rain, so only short dry grass species can survive there. The mixed-grass prairie grows in central Kansas. This region has both tall and short grasses. Some tall grasses grow in the mixed-grass prairie because it gets more rain than the short-grass prairie. The third major region is the tall-grass prairie. It grows in eastern Kansas, Iowa, and Illinois. This land receives more rain than either the short-grass or mixed-grass prairies. Some grass species that live here can reach heights of more than 10 feet (3 m)!

Canada rye grass, drooping coneflowers (left), and purple blazing star (right) grow on tall-grass prairies.

What Makes Prairies Unique?

Prairies are a unique habitat because they are flat, open spaces that do not provide much shelter. Prairie plants and animals are always exposed to harsh conditions.

Prairie climate changes with the seasons. In summer, temperatures can reach as high as 133° F (45°C). During winter, temperatures can fall below -49°F (-9°C).

Prairies receive little rain and are very dry. It is also quite windy because there are no natural barriers such as hills or forests to block the wind's path.

The combination of wind and dryness often leads to prairie fires. Lightning may spark fires that spread with the wind. Although fires burn the leaves and stems of plants, the roots and seeds survive underground. After rains, these plants grow again. They get nutrients from the ash the fire leaves behind.

Lightning **(right)** can cause prairie fires that burn the aboveground parts of plants, but roots and seeds survive underground so the plants can grow again **(inset)**.

Prairie Plants

Hundreds of species of grasses grow on a prairie. One thing that these prairie grasses have in common is that they have all adapted ways to survive the summer heat and dryness of the climate. Prairie grass leaves, called blades, have a needle-like shape. This shape keeps the plant from losing moisture. This is because only a small area of leaf is exposed to the drying sun and wind.

Left: The narrow leaves of this blue stem rye grass help it survive the dry prairie habitat. **Right:** Prairie plants have developed different ways to get water from deep in the soil.

Prairie grass roots grow in the cooler earth underground. This helps conserve moisture because the roots are not in contact with the sun and wind. An important job of these roots is to absorb and store water from the soil around them. Some species of grasses have long roots called tap roots. These roots can reach sources of water deep in the soil. Other species have shallow, matted roots that can soak up water close to the surface when it rains.

This black-eyed Susan has petals that gather dew for moisture.

Forbs are another type of plant that is very common on prairies. Forbs are non-grass, leafy plants such as wildflowers and herbs. Most forbs have small leaves with leathery or waxy surfaces. These coatings hold moisture in. Some plants have leaves with hairy surfaces that collect morning dew. This water then drips down to the soil, where the roots absorb the moisture.

Other plants besides grasses and forbs are found in the prairie habitat. Reeds, wild irises, and cattails grow beside ponds and streams in all three prairie regions. Mesquite and creosote bushes, and spiny cacti such as prickly pear cactus, live in drier short-grass regions.

Prickly pear cacti can store up water, which allows them to thrive in the driest prairies.

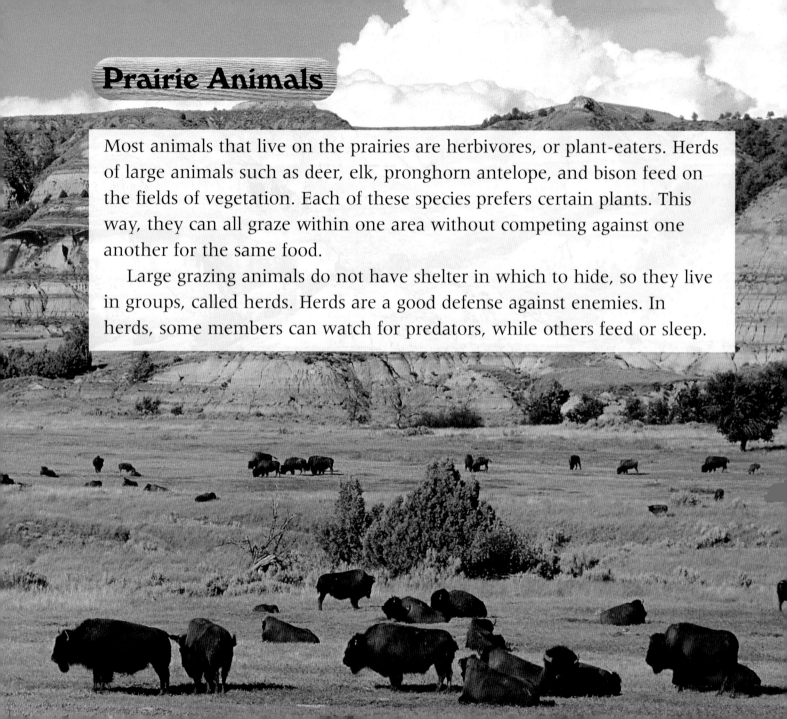

Prairie Animals

Most animals that live on the prairies are herbivores, or plant-eaters. Herds of large animals such as deer, elk, pronghorn antelope, and bison feed on the fields of vegetation. Each of these species prefers certain plants. This way, they can all graze within one area without competing against one another for the same food.

Large grazing animals do not have shelter in which to hide, so they live in groups, called herds. Herds are a good defense against enemies. In herds, some members can watch for predators, while others feed or sleep.

Since there are few hiding places on the prairie, many smaller animals dig holes called burrows. Burrows let these animals hide underground. Prairie dogs, which are a type of squirrel, are masters of this burrowing lifestyle. They are social animals that live together in large colonies call prairie dog towns.

Prairie dog towns are made up of a maze of burrows. They have several entrances. Prairie dogs keep vegetation clipped short near the entrances by biting off plants that might interfere with a clear view of approaching predators.

Left: Bison graze in a herd to protect themselves from predators on the open prairie. **Right:** Prairie dogs live in a underground mazes of burrows called prairie dog towns.

Prairie dogs are always alert for predators such as hawks, owls, badgers, foxes, and coyotes when they leave their burrows to feed. A few of the prairie dogs act like scouts. They stand watch on their hind legs, while the others eat. If a prairie dog senses danger, it gives a bark-like warning or a loud whistle and all of the prairie dogs run for the safety of their burrows.

Prairie dogs eat grasses and seeds. Rabbits nibble on grass, shrubs, and leafy plants. Smaller animals such as shrews, mice, and ground squirrels collect seeds and grass grains to prepare for the long winter. They store them in their holes below the ground.

A prairie dog scout whistles a warning to other prairie dogs Other small animals like this rabbit (inset) must be just as careful.

Insects are even smaller plant-eaters that live on the prairies. Grasshoppers feed on blades of grass, and butterflies and bees sip nectar from the prairie wildflowers. Large predatory insects such as dragonflies, praying mantises, and spiders also make the grasslands their home. They prey on smaller, plant-eating insects.

Birds are another type of small predator found on the prairies. Quail, prairie chickens, and pheasants feed on insects along the ground. Songbirds catch insects that fly through the air. Sharp-clawed hawks and owls prey on mice, baby birds, prairie dogs, and ground squirrels.

Grasshoppers feed on prairie grasses (top) while monarch butterflies (bottom) drink nectar from flowers for nourishment.

17

Prairies are also home to a number of other predators such as snakes, badgers, and weasels. They feed on the same animals that hawks and owls hunt. All of these small predators are important because they keep the populations of prey balanced.

Coyotes, foxes, and bobcats are the main large predators on the prairies. They feed on deer, elk, and pronghorn antelope. These predators have evolved into fast runners to catch their speedy prey. Coyotes and swift foxes can sprint at speeds of more than 40 mph (67 km/h). Wolves work together in packs like relay racers. They take turns chasing their prey. This helps them tire out antelope and even bring down adult bison.

Scavengers are another important group of animals that live on the prairies. Scavengers such as turkey vultures and ravens feed on dead animals. Beetles, worms, and millipedes then break down the remaining scraps, which helps to keep the prairie habitat clean.

Badgers **(inset)** and coyote are just two predators that keep the prairie population balanced.

Food Chain

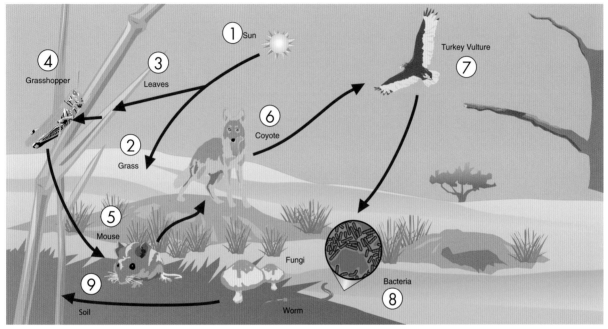

The food chain shows a step-by-step example of how energy in the prairie habitat is exchanged through food: sunlight **(1)** is used by grass **(2)** to make sugar, which is then stored in its leaves **(3)**, shoots, roots, and seeds. When a grasshopper **(4)** eats grass, some of the plant's energy becomes part of the grasshopper. When the grasshopper is eaten by a mouse **(5)**, which in turn is eaten by a coyote **(6)**, the energy is passed from creature to creature. When the coyote dies, scavengers such as turkey vultures **(7)** and insects dispose of the waste and gain energy for themselves. Decomposers, such as fungi and bacteria **(8)**, break down and become part of the soil **(9)**. Plants use their roots to absorb this nutrition in addition to the energy that their leaves receive from the sun. Then the whole cycle begins again.

Humans and Prairies

Over the centuries, prairie land has been taken up by towns, roads, agriculture, and grazing livestock. Today, only small areas of natural prairie habitat remain.

One way to protect the remaining pieces of wild prairie land is to preserve it. Conservation organizations buy prairie land. They do not allow farms, roads, or towns to be built there. With such protection, native grasses have the chance to grow back, and the populations of endangered animals may have a chance to increase.

The Prairie Learning Center in Iowa's Neal Smith National Wildlife Refuge teaches people how to preserve America's prairies.

This volunteer teaches his son how to handle plants from a tall-grass prairie.

People will never be able to return to the days when wild prairies stretched endlessly across North America, But humans can help preserve and protect the remaining wild prairie habitats for future generations.

A Prairies's Food Web

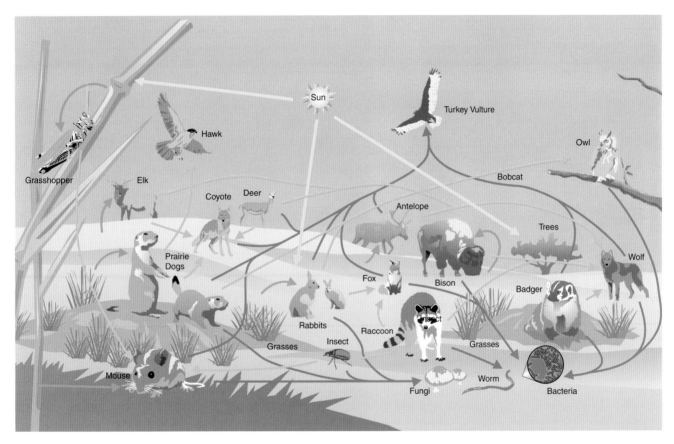

Food webs show how creatures in a habitat depend on one another to survive. The arrows in this drawing show the flow of energy from one creature to another. Yellow arrows: green plants which make food from air and sunlight; Green arrows: animals that eat the green plants; Orange arrows: predators; Red arrows: scavengers and decomposers. These reduce dead bodies to their basic chemicals, which return to the soil to be taken up by green plants, beginning the cycle all over again.

2103877

Glossary

Burrow A tunnel or hole in the ground that an animal digs for its home or shelter

Decomposers Animals such as earthworms and plants such as fungi, that eat dead tissue and return nutrients to the soil.

Forb A forb is the name given to non-grass, leafy plants such as herbs and wildflowers that do not have woody stems or bark like trees and shrubs do.

Habitat The area in which a plant or animal naturally lives. Habitat provides living organisms with everything they need to survive—food, water, and shelter.

Herbivores Animals such as deer, that get their food and energy by eating only plants.

Mixed-grass prairie The part of the prairie between the western and eastern prairie. Both short grasses and tall grasses grow here.

Short-grass prairie The western, dry prairie where grasses grow up to two feet tall.

Tall-grass prairie The eastern prairie that receives the most rainfall. Here grasses can grow over ten feet tall.

For Further Reading

Books

Bauer, Erwin A., and Peggy Bauer. *Save our Prairies and Grasslands.* New York: Delacorte Press, 1994.

Patent, Dorothy. *Prairies.* New York: Holiday House, 1996.

Stille, Darlene R. *Grasslands.* New York: Childrens Press, 1999.

Websites

Northern Prairie Biological Resources
http://www.npwrc.usgs.gov/resource/resource.htm

Meadowbrook Prairie
http://www.prairienet.org/meadowbrook

Pawnee National Grassland
http://www.fs.fed.us/arnf/png

Index

Adaptation, 10
Animals, 8, 14-19, 21, 23

Birds, 17
Burrows, 14

Climate, 8, 10

Energy, 20, 23
Environment, 21-22

Fires, 8
Food chain, 20
Food web, 23
Forbs, 13

Grasses, 4, 7, 10-11, 20

Habitats, 4, 8, 21, 23
Herbivores, 14
Herbs, 13

Herds, 14
Humans, 21-22

Insects, 17

Lightning, 8

Mixed-grass prairie, 7

Plants, 8, 10-13, 20, 23
Prairie dogs, 15-16

Predators, 14, 15-16, 17, 18, 23

Rain, 8

Scavengers, 18, 23
Short-grass prairie, 7, 13

Tall-grass prairie, 7

Wildflowers, 4, 13
Wind, 8, 11

J577.44

2-5

2103877

DISCARDED

AUG 2004

Barberton Public Library
602 West Park Avenue
Barberton, Ohio 44203-2458
(303) 745-1194

330

DEMCO

BARBERTON PUBLIC LIBRARY BARBERTON, OHIO